I0189903

www.ingramcontent.com/pod-product-compliance
Lightning Source LLC
Chambersburg PA
CBHW081242020426
42331CB00013B/3275

9 780992 758684

easy alef-bet

by Linda Samuels B.A.

Note to the teacher:

This book can be used with young English-speaking children as an introduction to Hebrew letters and sounds. The mnemonic beneath each letter may give an added clue to remembering the letter eg., Hay has a stick ; Pay has a parcel etc.

This book has also proved to be an easy way for adults to learn to read Hebrew.

Pato Press
P O Box 70114
London
N12 2DT

British Library Cataloguing-in-Publication Data
A catalogue record for this eBook is available
from the British Library.
ISBN: 978-0-9927586-8-4

Visit us on the World Wide Web at:
www.patopress.com

Kindle edition published 2015 by Pato Press

Book Design and Production
Basil Samuels and Clare O Hagan
Printed by CreateSpace

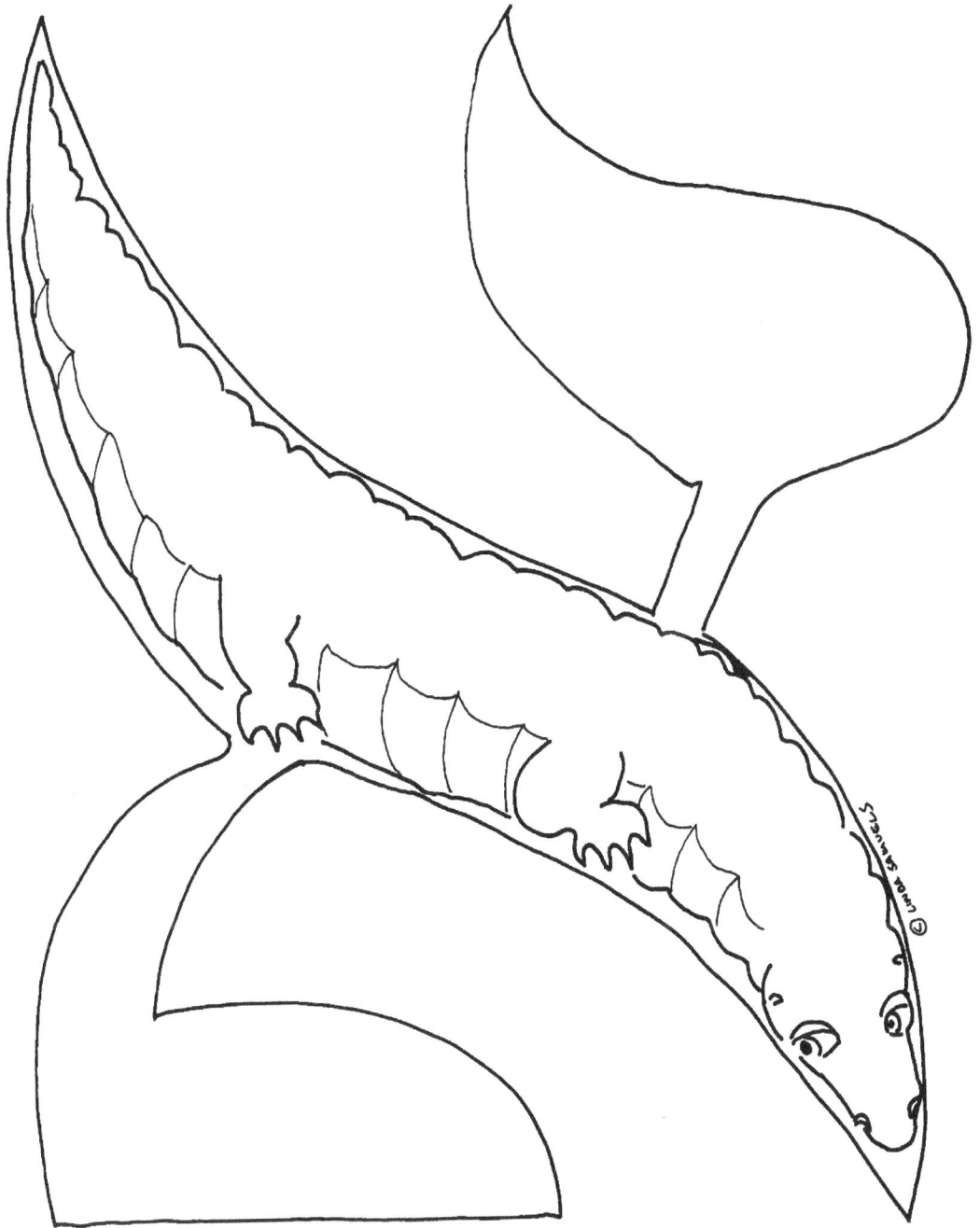

Ally **Alef** keeps his mouth shut and says nothing. Luckily for us!

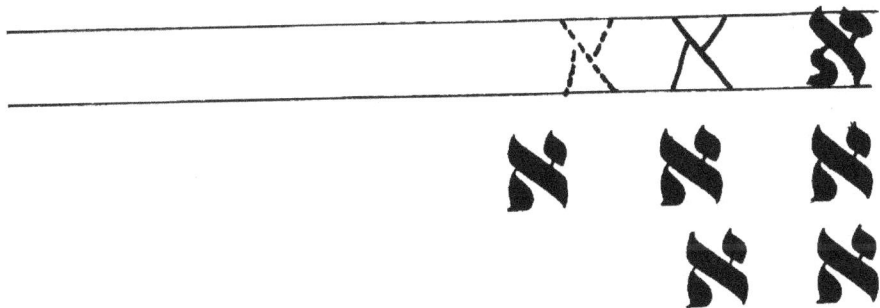

Vowel Owl
gives you vowel sounds

These two signs

— ⊤

sound like
u̲ as in cu̲p

They go under letters

Now you can
make a sound.

2

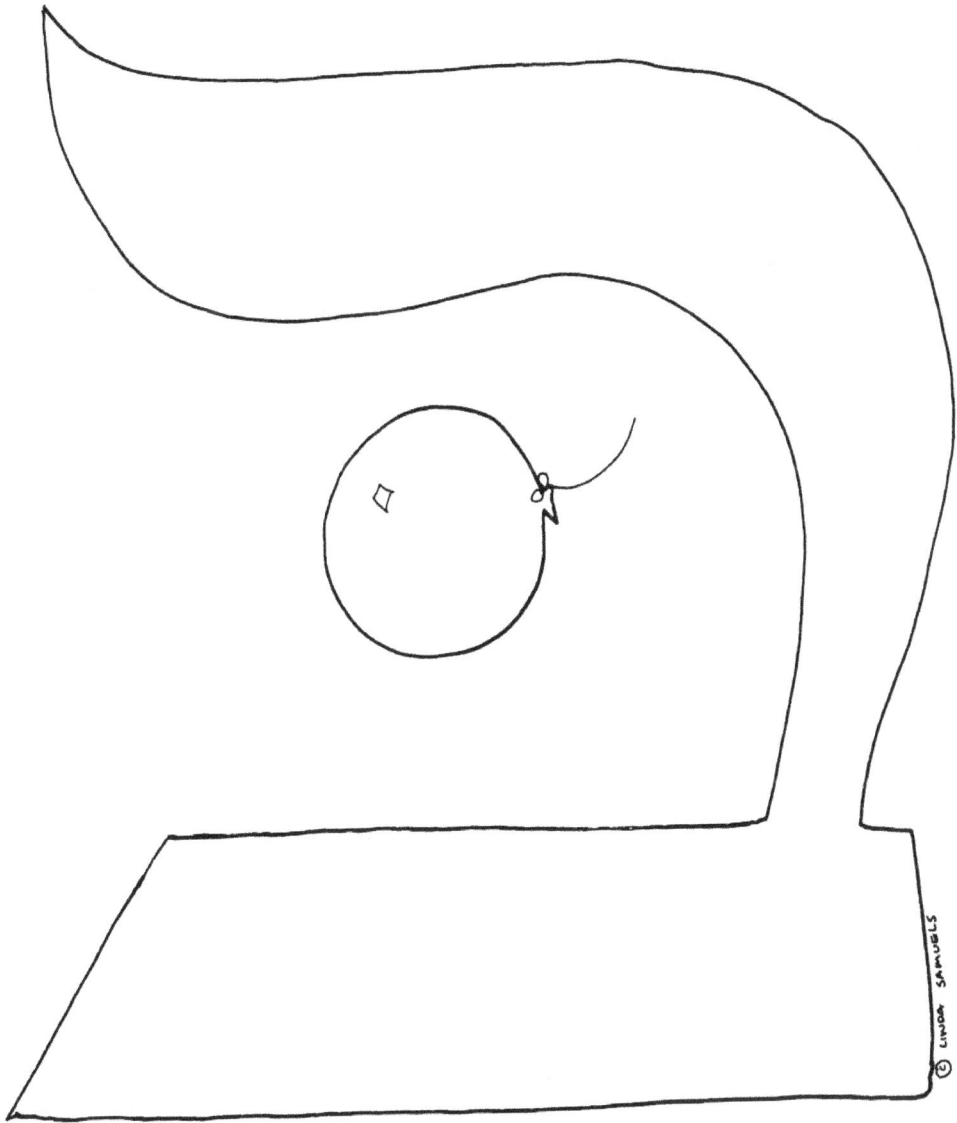

Balloony **Bet** blows balloons

בּ בָּ בָ בְּ בֵ

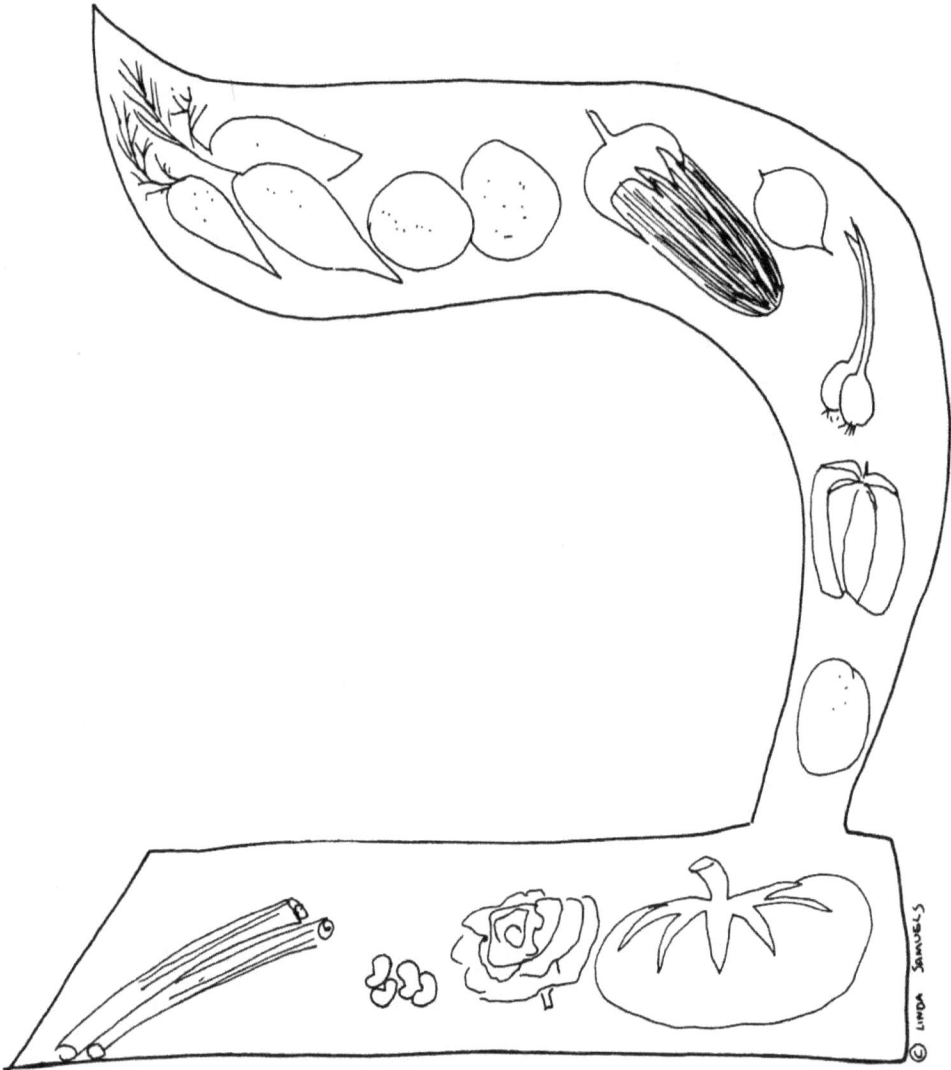

Vegetable **Vet** values vitamins

בּ

בְּ בְּ בְּ בְּ בַּ

Vowel Owl gives you _____ •

it sounds like i̱ as in li̱ps ki̱ss
it also goes under the letters

now try

בּ בּ אִ

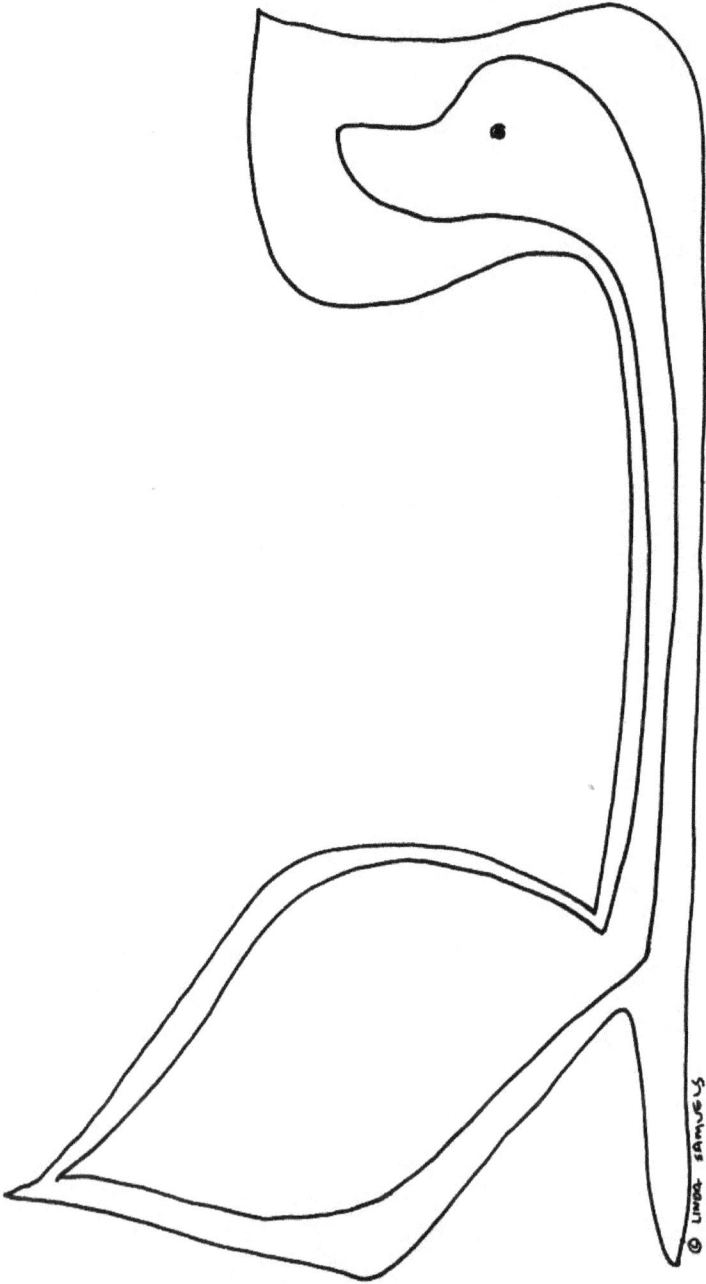

Goosey **Gimmel** giggles

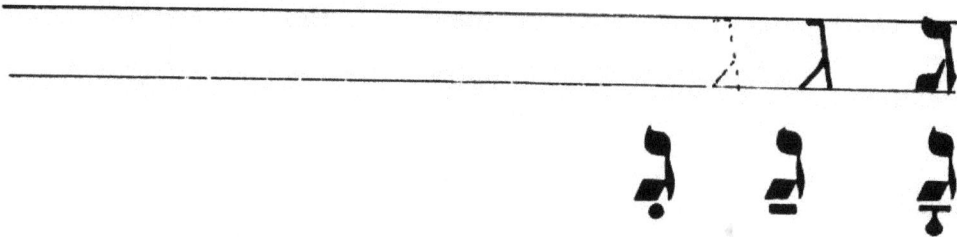

ג ג ג

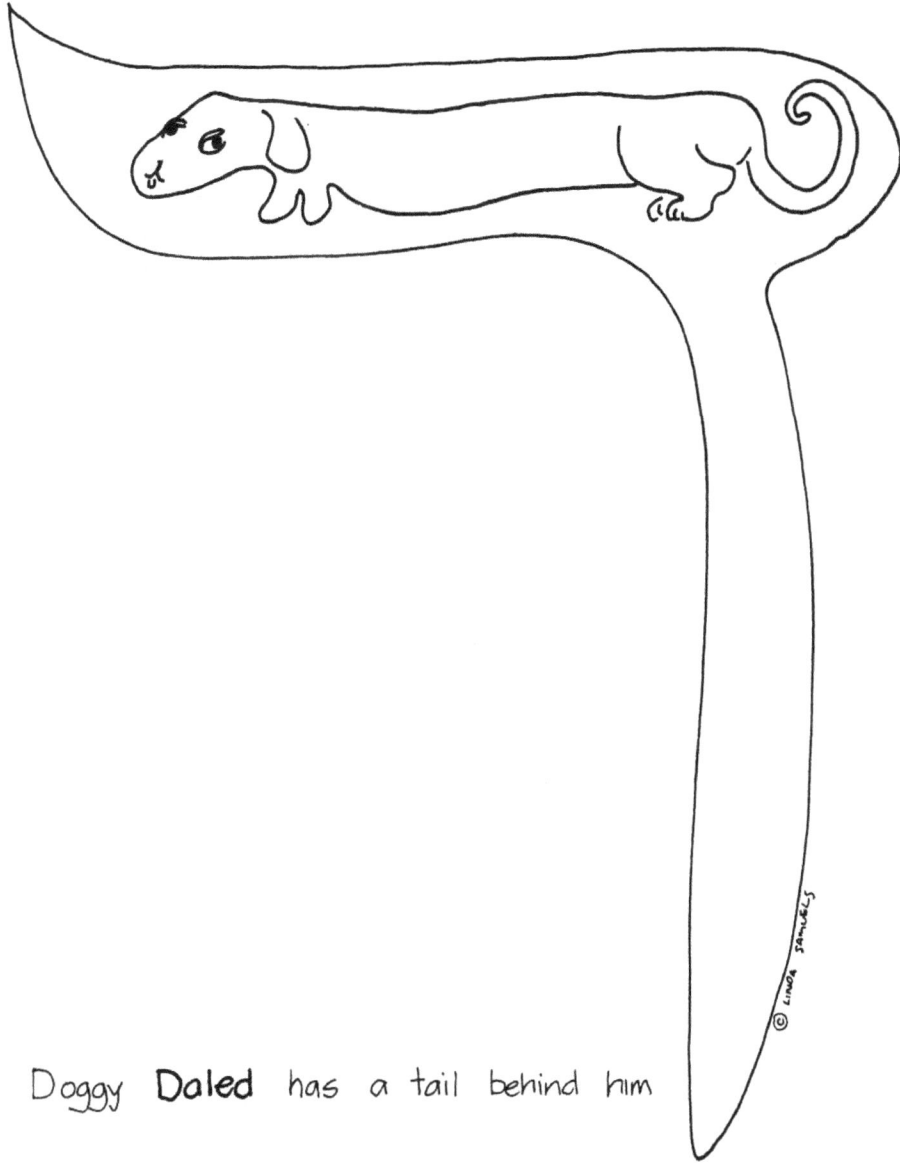

Doggy **Daled** has a tail behind him

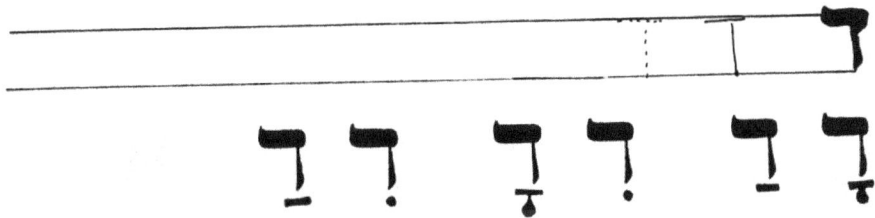

ד   ד   דּ   דִ   דֻ   דְ
          דֹ   דֳ   דֶ   דַ

Vowel Owl gives you _____
          ⟍•
          •⟍•

it also goes under the letters

it sounds like e̲ as in e̲ggs

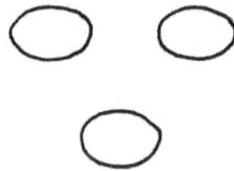

אֶ בֶּ גֶּ דֶּ

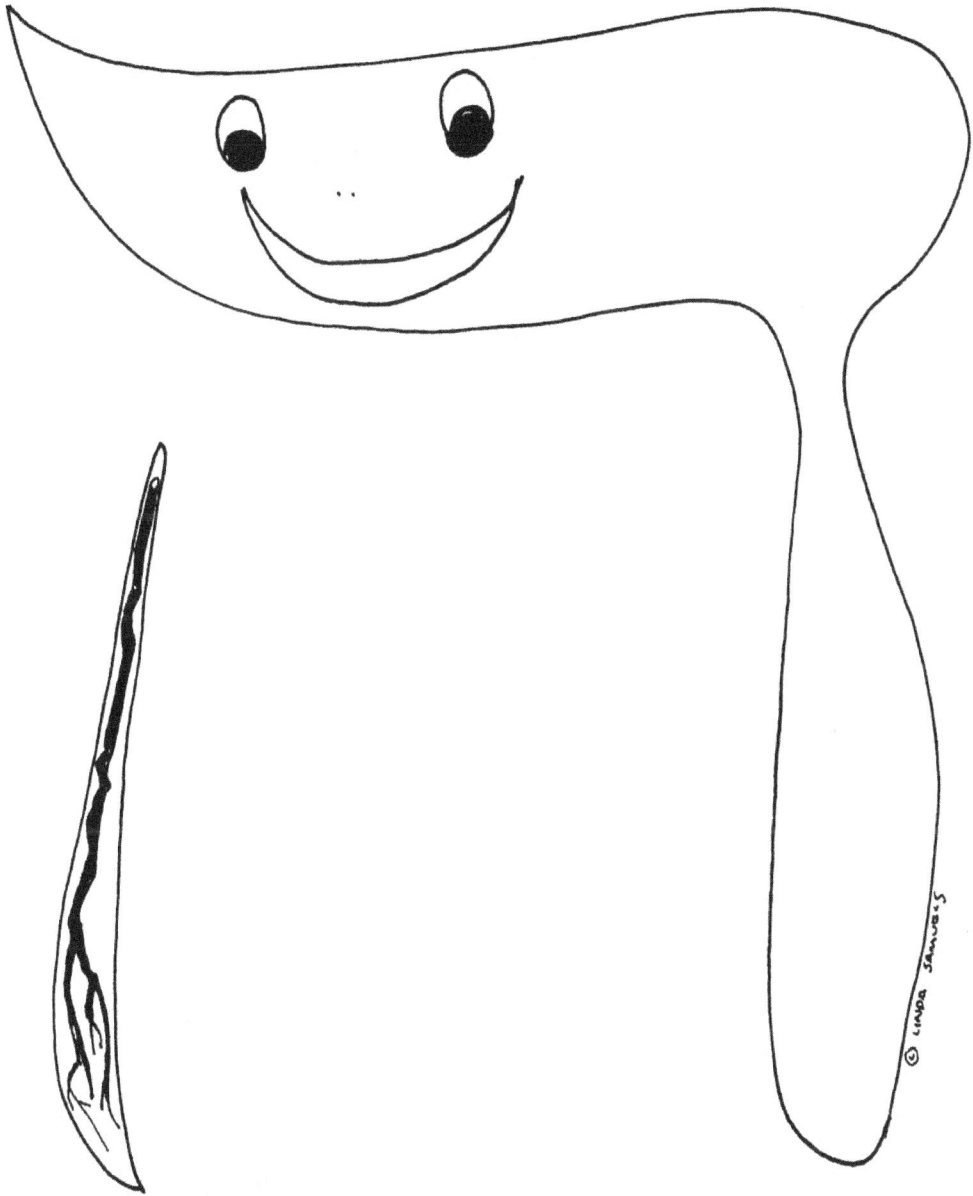

Happy **Hay** has a handy stick

ה

הֵ הָ הִ הְ

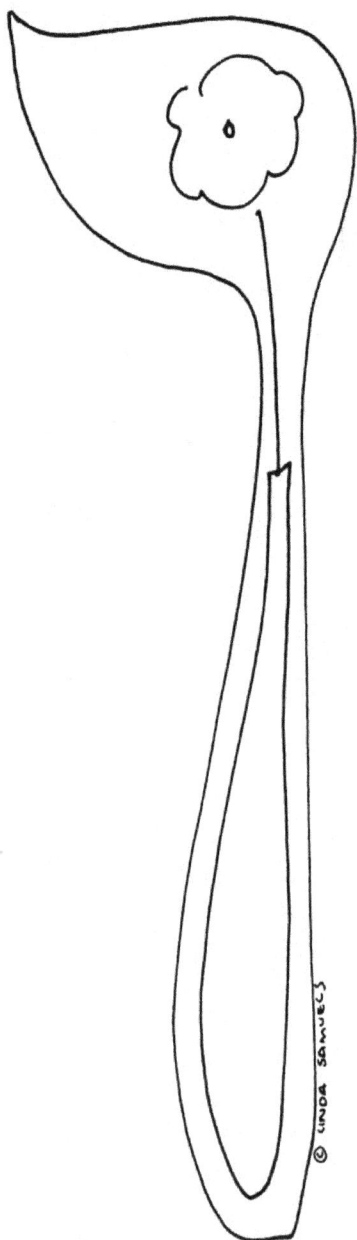

Vase **Vav** is very thin

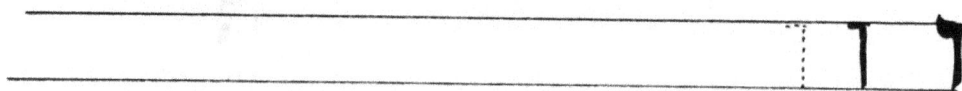

Vowel Owl now gives you _____ •••

which sounds like <u>oo</u> as in m<u>oo</u>

אֻבֻּגֻדֻהֻוֻ

11

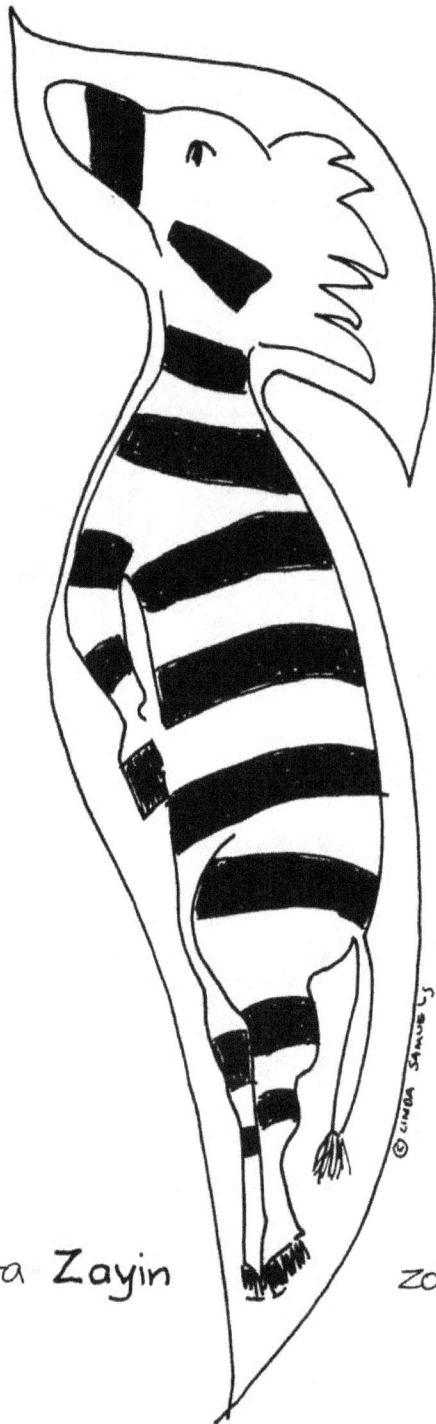

Zebra Zayin   zooms up

Challa **Chet** is next to tet

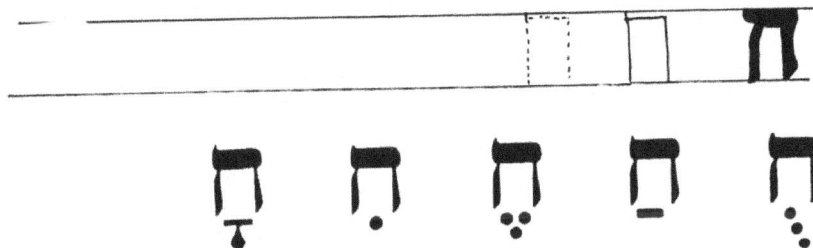

חַ חֲ חֱ חִ חַ

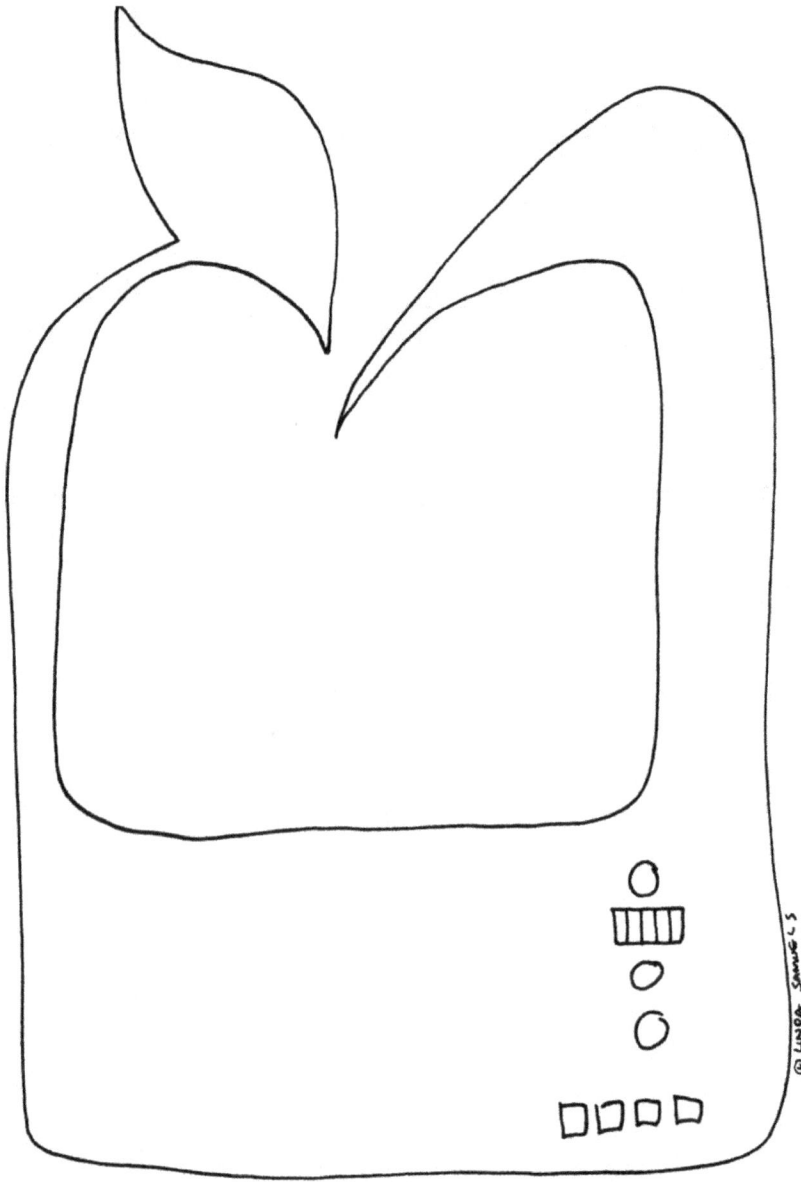

Telly **Tet** turns on too much T.V.

ט   ט   טֻ

טָ   טֶ   טִ   טֹ   טֻ

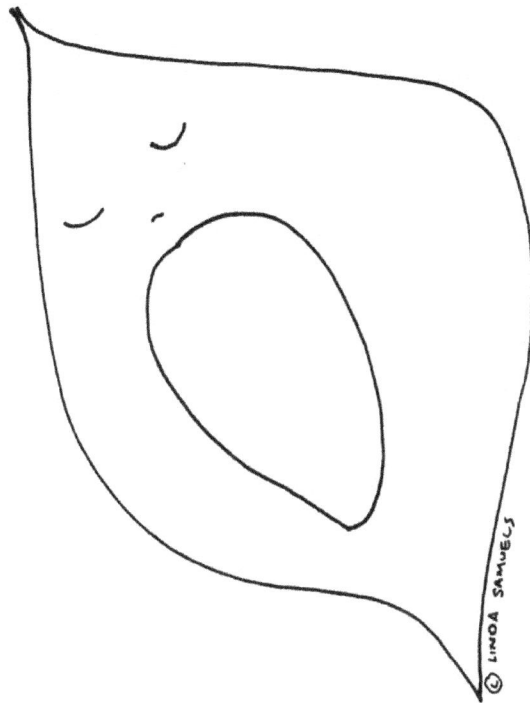

Yawning **Yud** floats up to bed

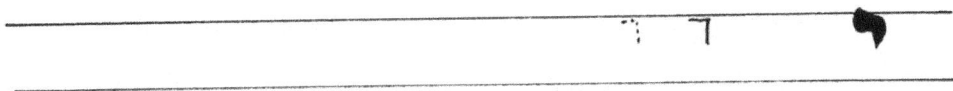

Vowel Owl says

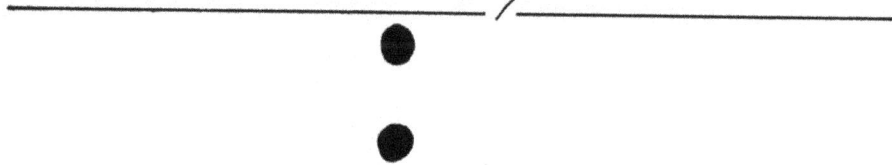

אָ בְּ בְּ גְּ דְּ הְּ וְּ
זְּ חְּ טְ יְ

This allows the letter to sound by itself
It goes under the letter too.

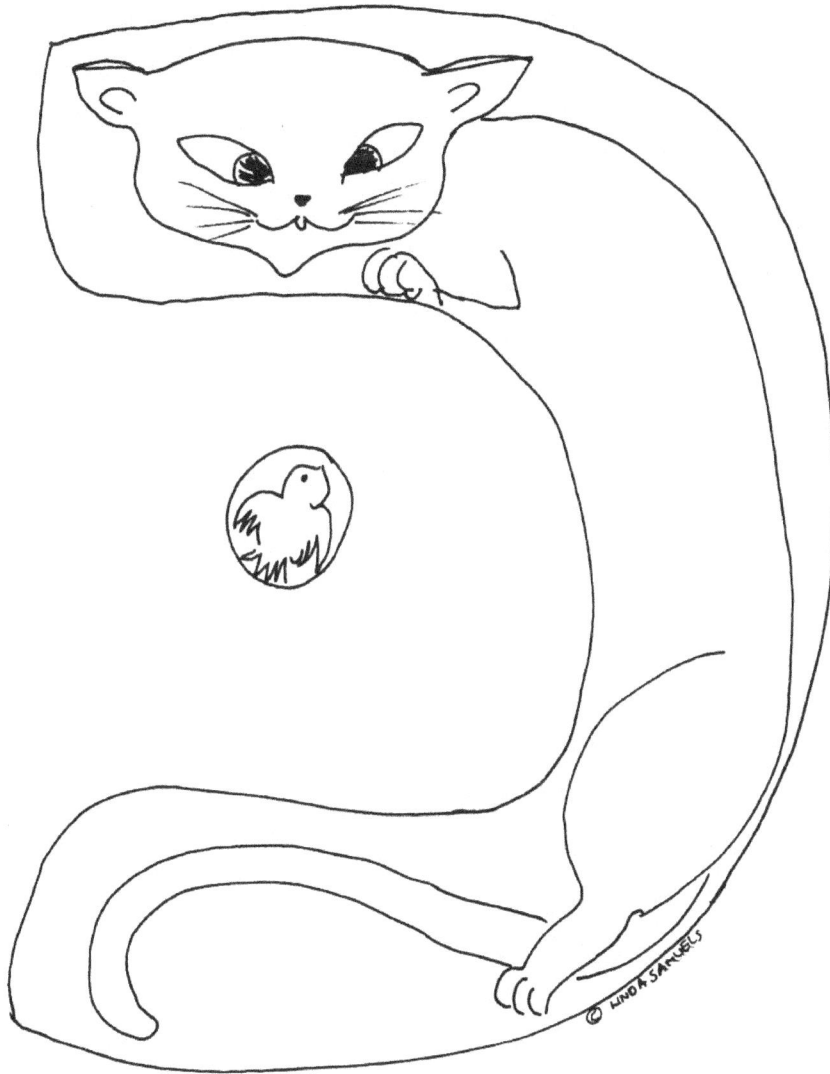

Catty **Caf** catches a canary

כְּ כָּ כַּ כֻּ כּ

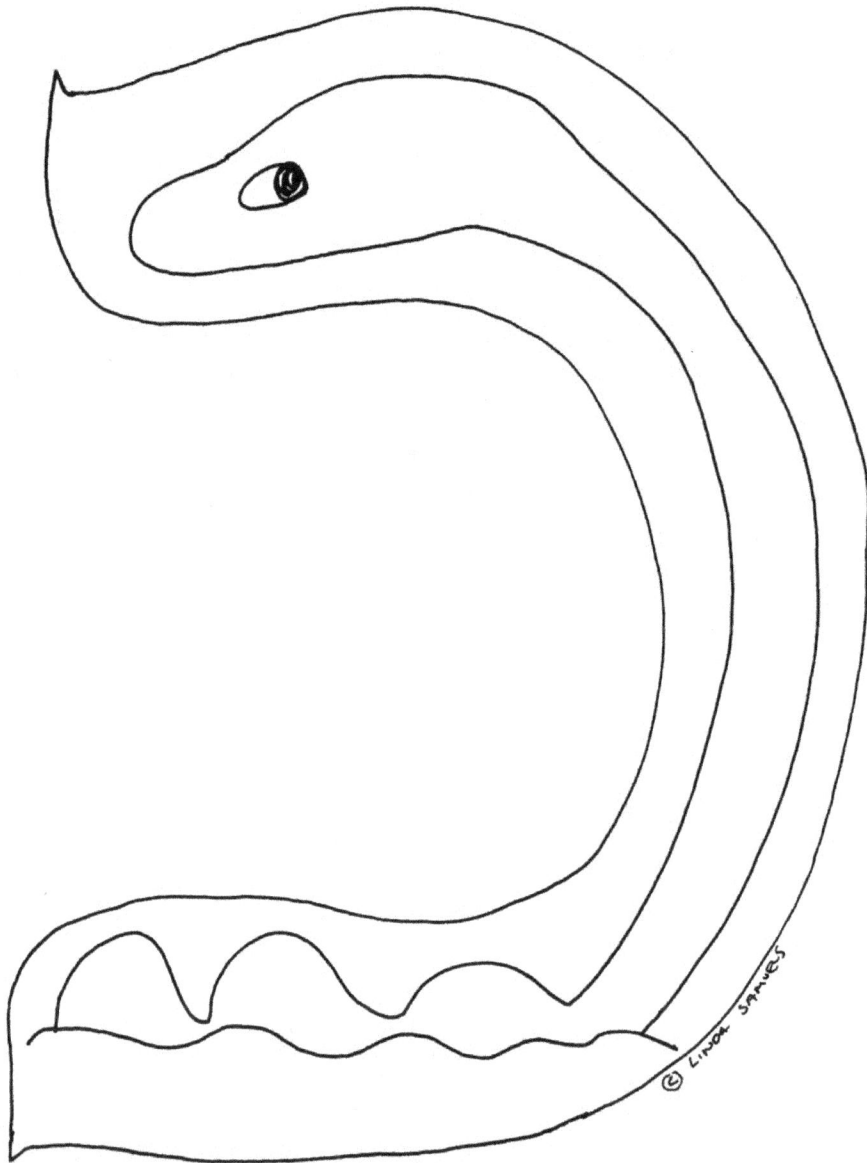

Lo<u>ch</u> ness <u>Ch</u>af

כ כ כ כ כ

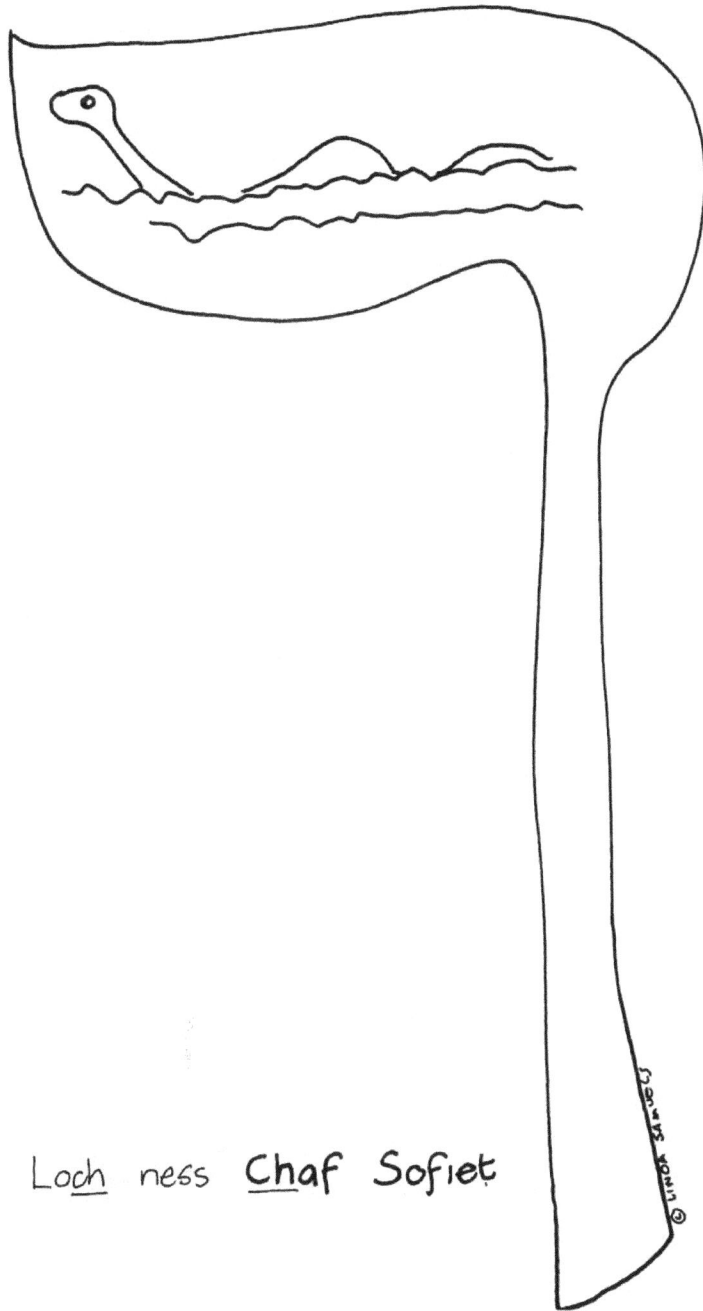

Lo<u>ch</u> ness **<u>Ch</u>af Sofiet** ends his swim

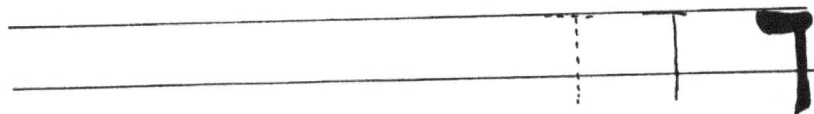

כַּ אַ בַּ

ך

Vowel Owl gives you

• and וֹ

which sound like the o as in dot on top

אוֹ בּוֹ בוֹ גוֹ דוֹ הוֹ

זוֹ חוֹ טוֹ

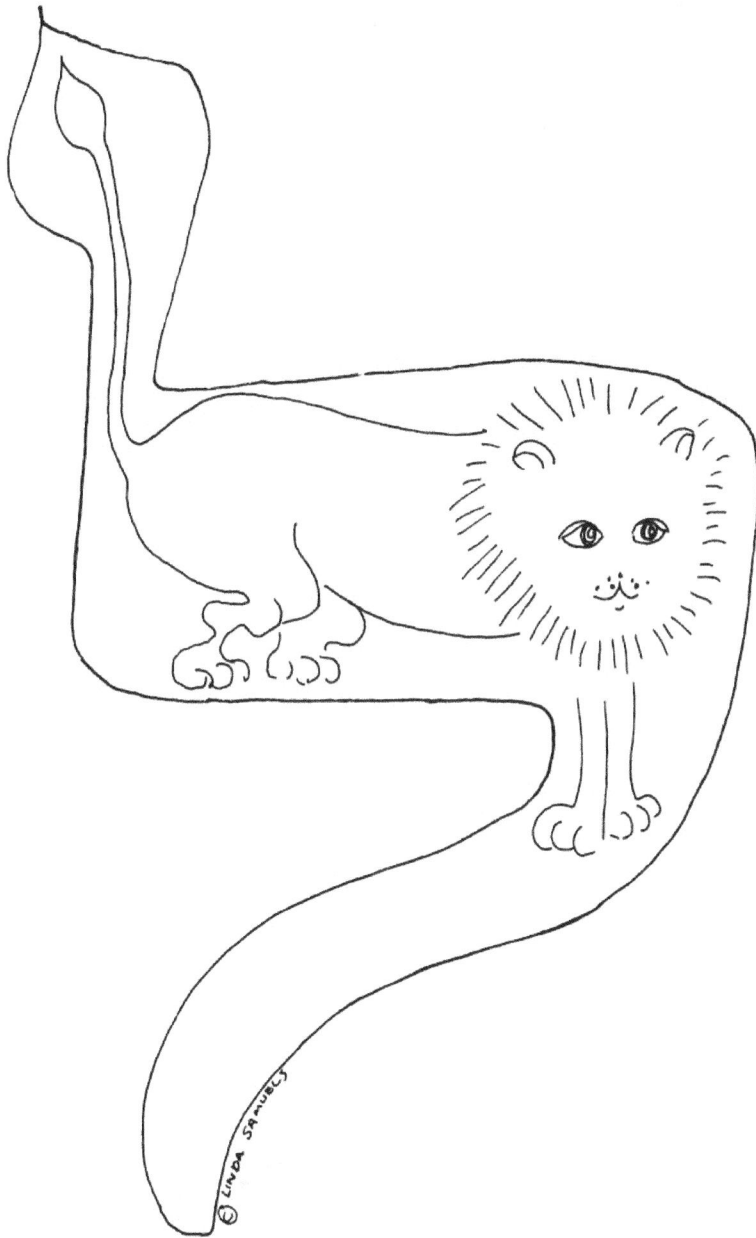

Lion **Lamed** leaps and lopes

Vowel Owl now gives you ___ which sounds like <u>a</u> in gate

אֵ בֵּ גֵ דֵ הֵ הֵ
זֵ חֵ טֵ יֵ כֵ כֵ לֵ

22

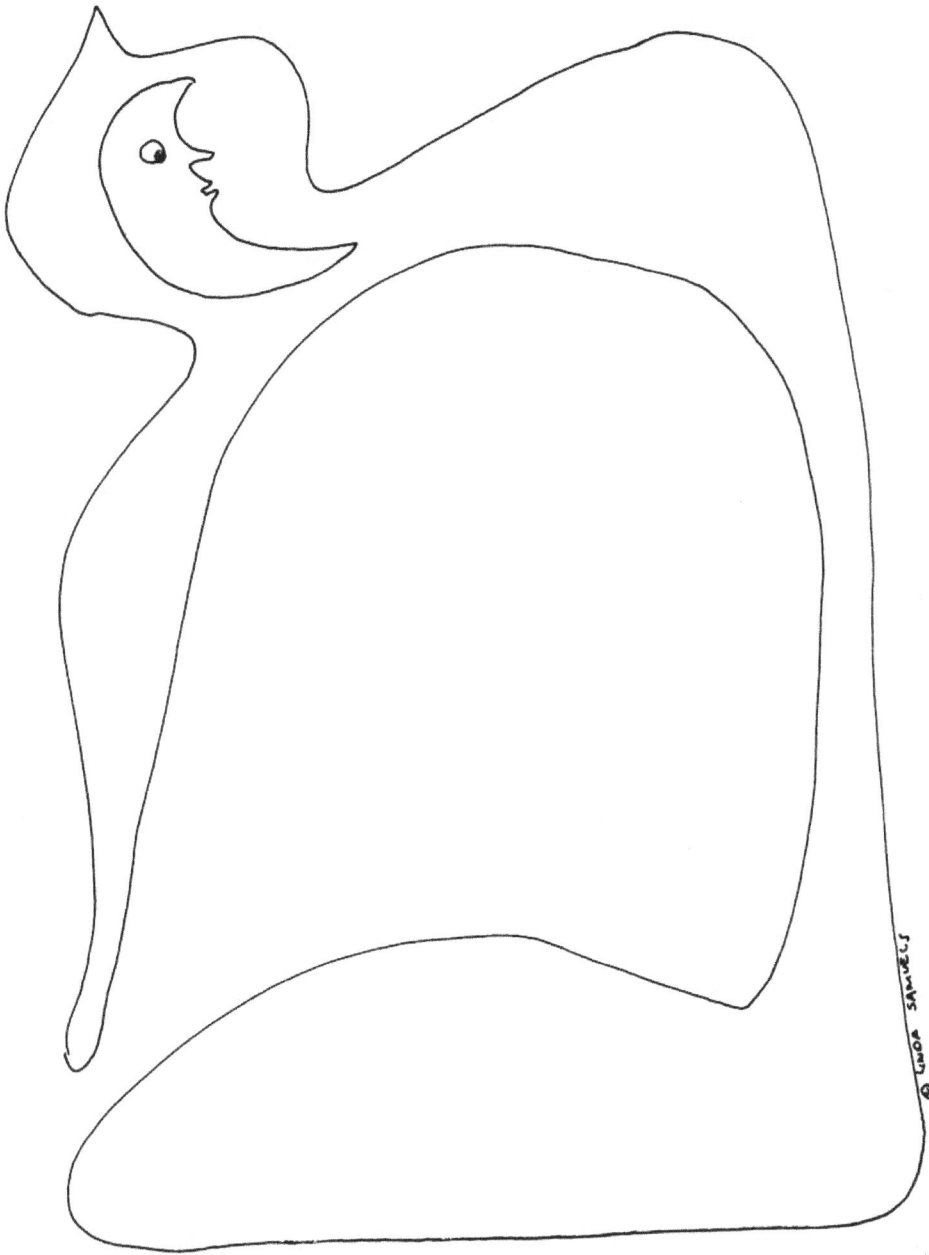

Moony **Mem** is awake for the night

מ

מִ מֻ מֶ מָ מוֹ מֵ מְ

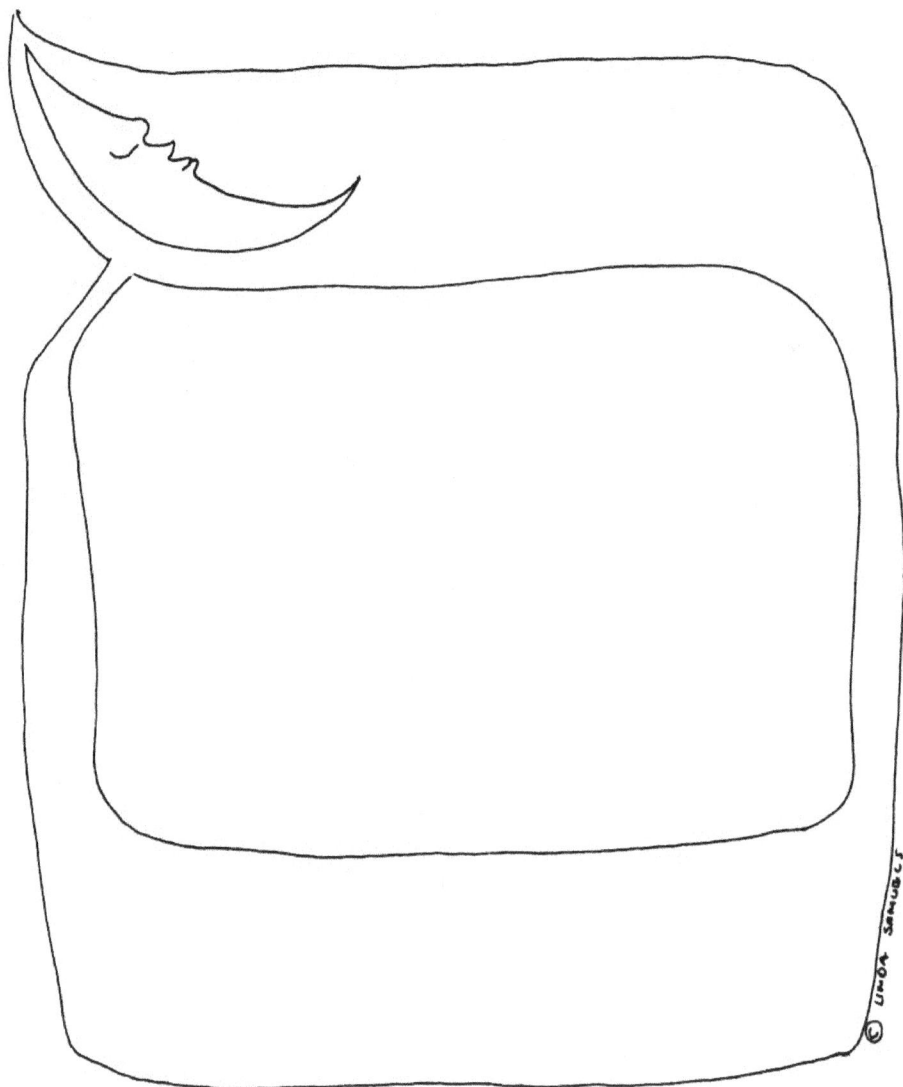

Moony **Mem Sofiet** is closed up for the day

Vowel Owl gives
you another oo

as in Tu - wit tu woo that ball might hit you!

אוּ בּוּ בוּ דוּ
לוּ מוּ

Naily **Nun** needs nothing

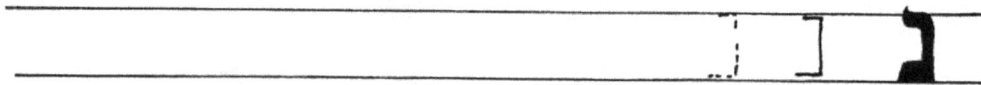

נַ נֶ נֹ נְ נָ

נִ נוּ נֻ נֵ

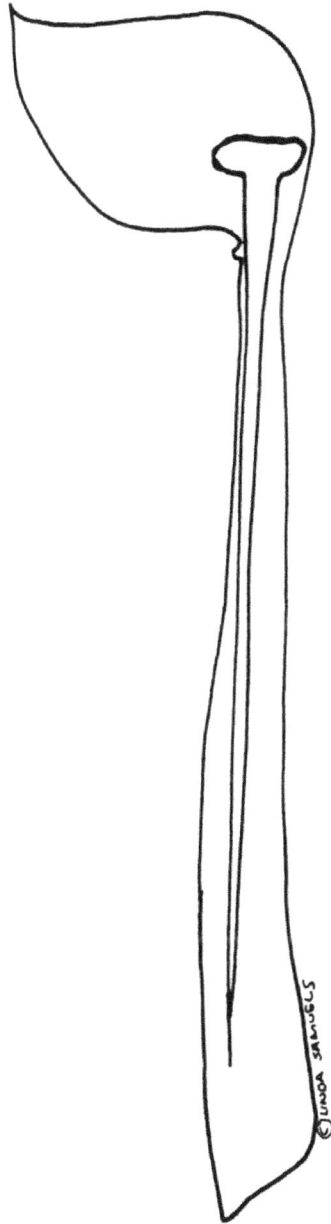

Naily **Nun Sofiet** needs to finish

ן

בֵּן בֵּן

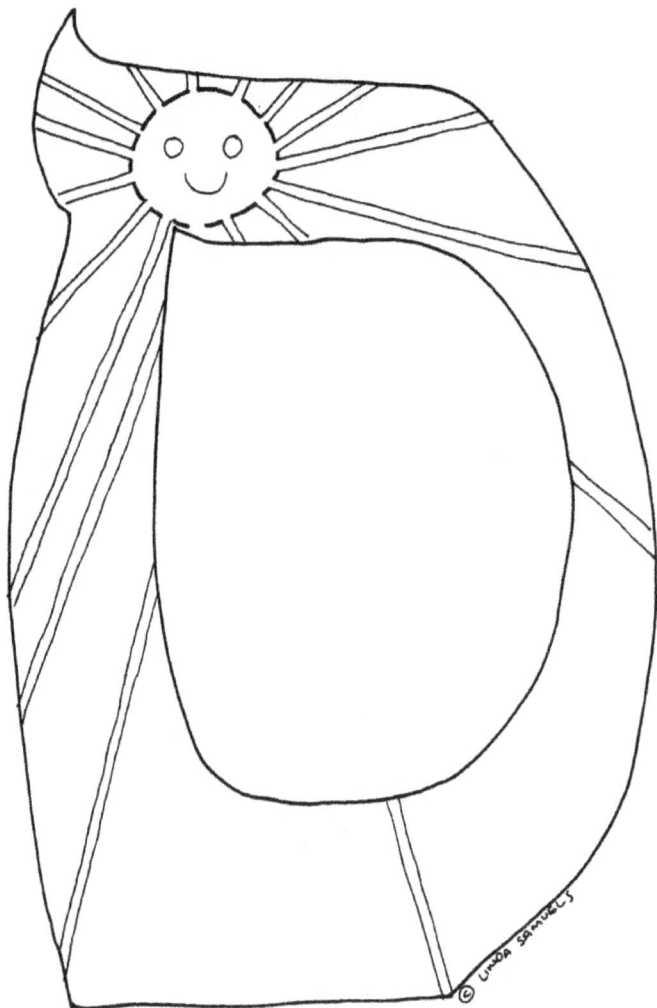

Sunny **Samech** smiles around

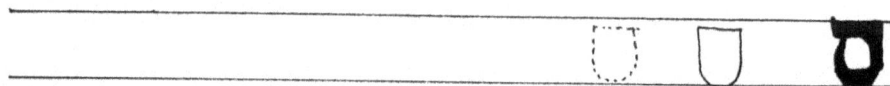

סוֹ סוּ סִי סֹ

סְ סֵ סֶ סַ

Vowel Owl now gives you ___ בְ

© LINDA SAMUELS

sounds like <u>ey</u> as in k<u>ey</u>

אִי בִּי גִּי דִי הִי זִי חִי
טִי כִּי לִי מִי נִי סִי

29

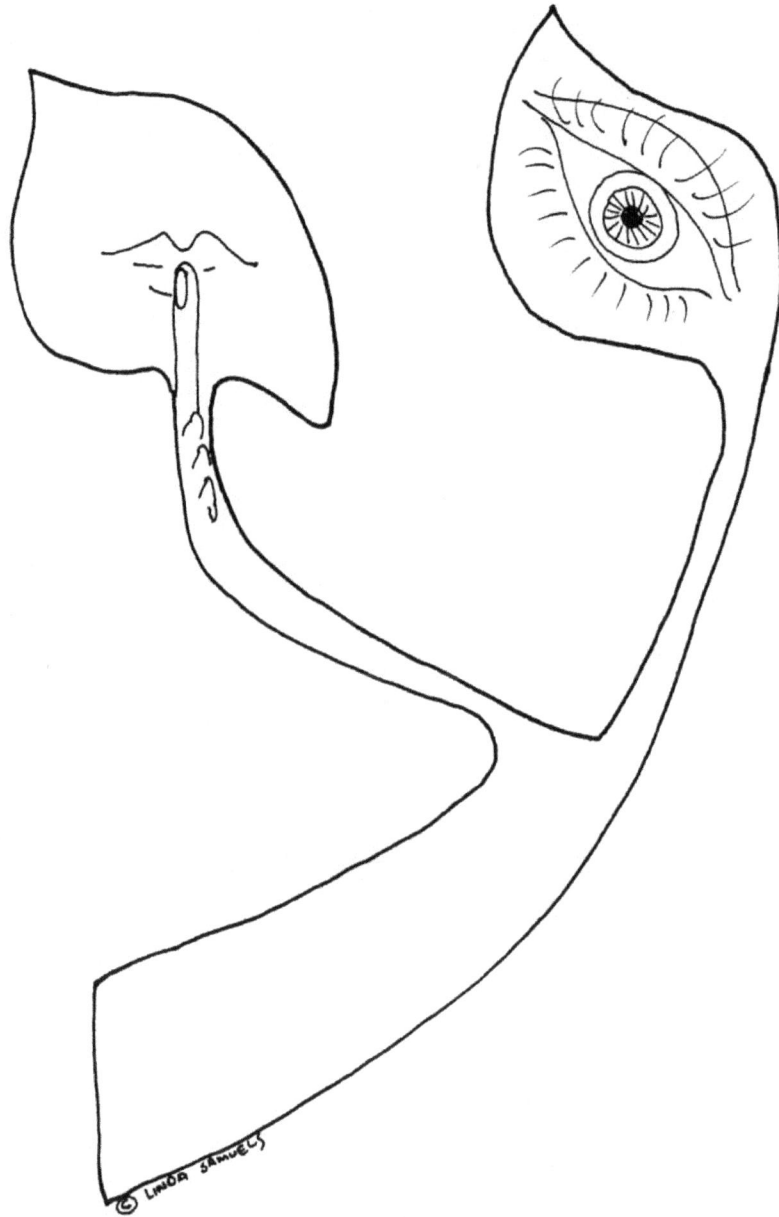

Eyeing **Ayin** sees but does not speak

עְ עֶ עִ עַ עָ

עָ עַ עֻ עֹ עֵ

Postman **Pay** has a parcel

פַ | פּ ⌐•⌐ | •⌐•

פִּי | פֶּ | פֵּ | פָ

פֶּ | פּוֹ | פּוּ | פֹּ

31

Flowery **Fay** flies near Pay

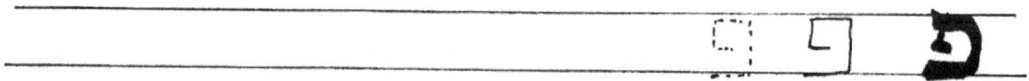

פ   פ   פ

פֵ   פִי   פֵ   פֶ

פוֹ   פַ   פָ   פֻ

Flowery **Fay Sofiet** ends the story

ף ך

אַף דַף

Vowel Owl gives you _____ יֵ

sounds like <u>ay</u> as in p<u>ay</u>

אֵי בֵּי גֵּי דֵי הֵי וֵי זֵי חֵי טֵי
יֵי כֵּי כֵי לֵי מֵי נֵי סֵי עֵי פֵּי פֵי

34

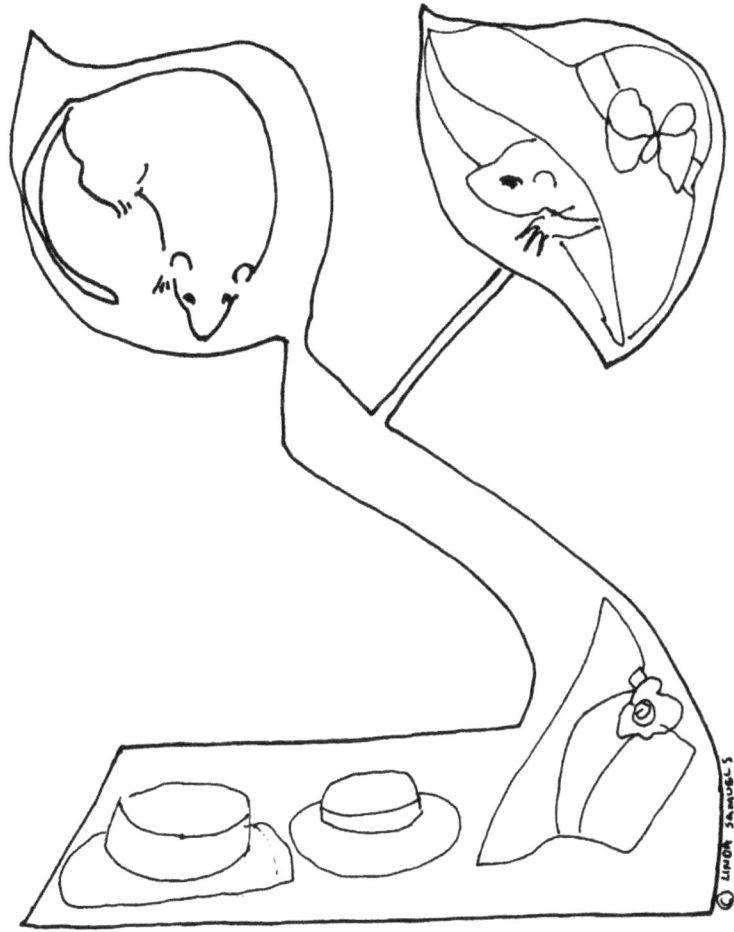

Tzadi has ra<u>ts</u> and ha<u>ts</u>

צֲ   צֶ   צִ   צָ   צַ

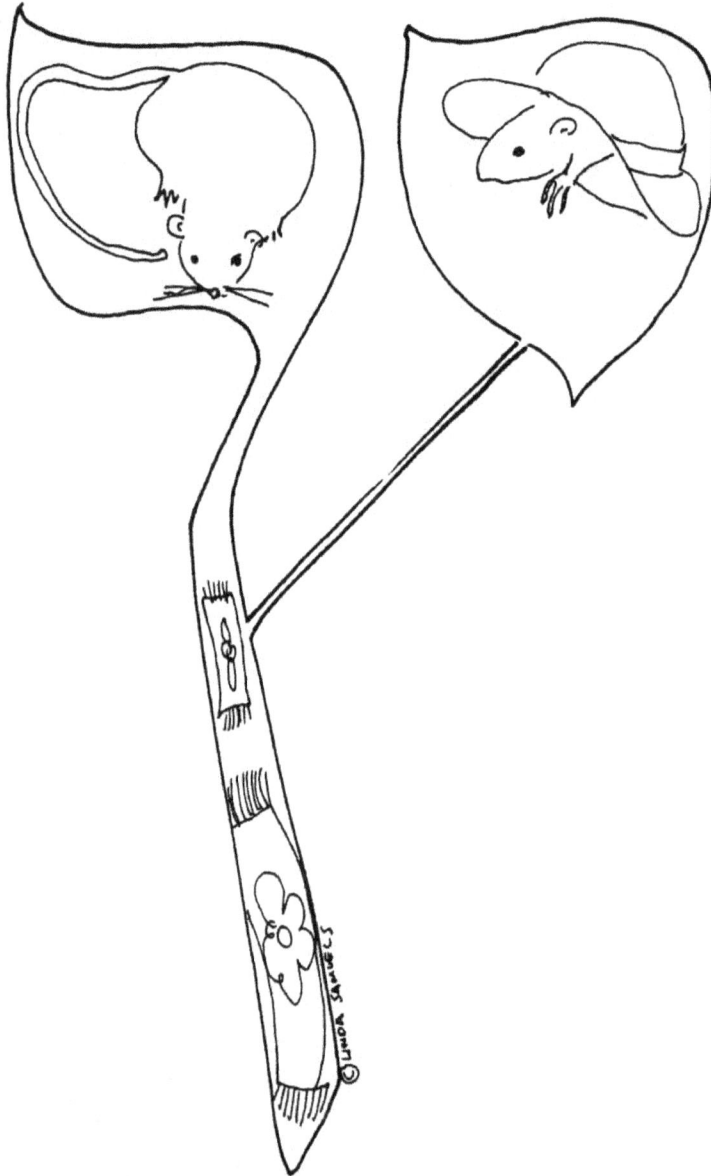

Tzadi Sofiet has ra<u>ts</u> ha<u>ts</u> and ma<u>ts</u>

ץ

צֵץ לֵץ עֵץ

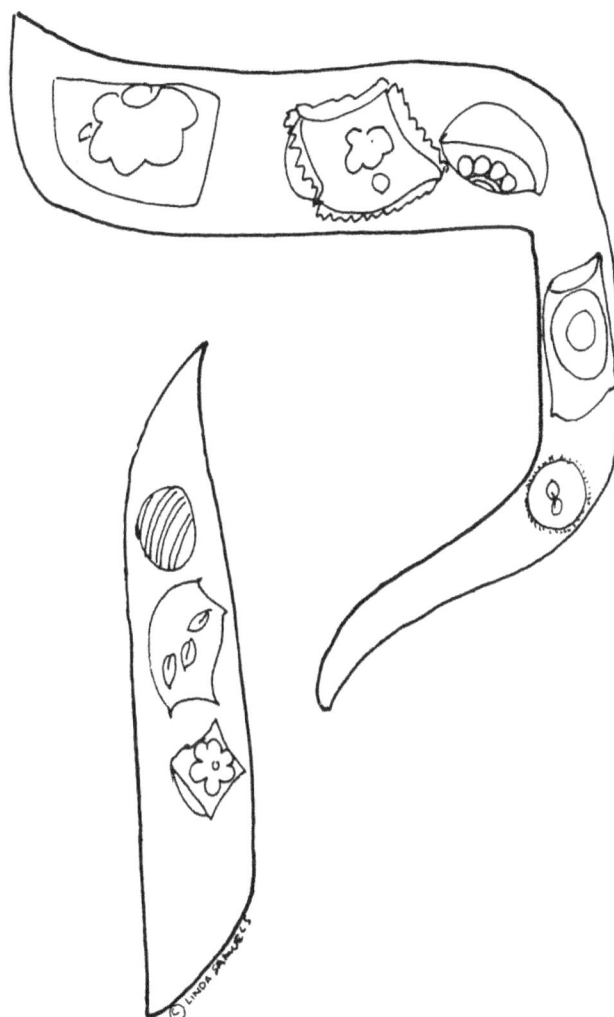

Cushy **Koof** cuddles up

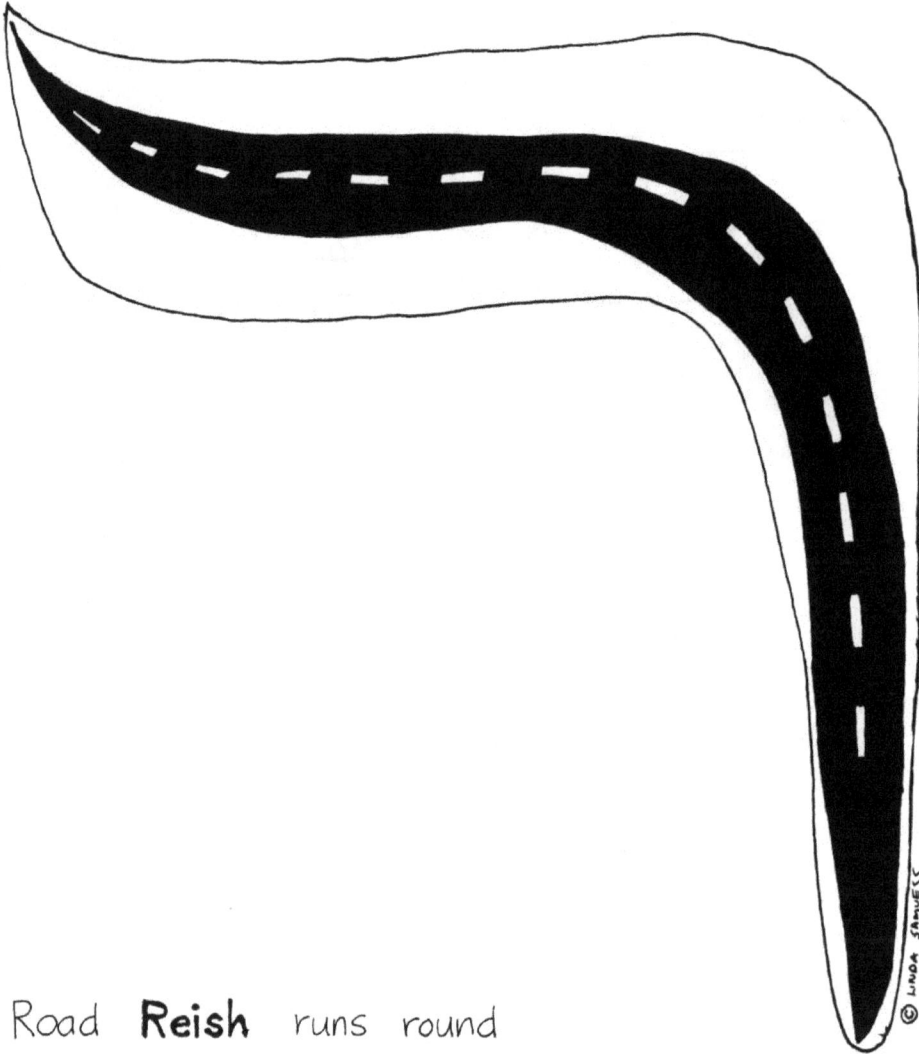

Road **Reish** runs round

ר ר ֶ ר ְ ר ִ ר ַ

Shiny **Shin** is right and bright

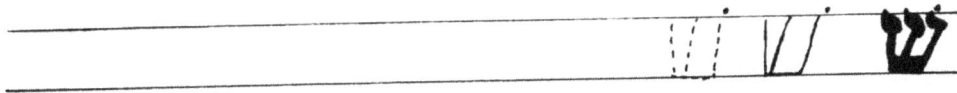

שִׁ שִׁ שִׁ שֶׁךְ
שָׁ שִׁ שֵׁ שֵׁי

Silver **Sin** is on the left

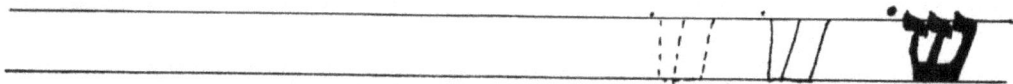

שׂוֹ שֶׁ שֶׁ שֵׁר
שֵׂ שֶׁ שֵׁ שֵׁ שַׂ

Tubby **Tav** and his terrific tea

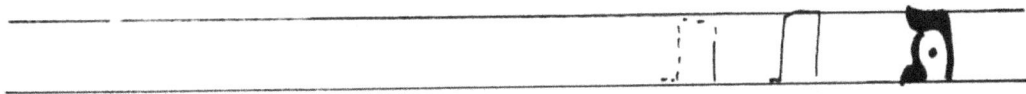

תָּ תָ תַ תֵ תֶ תִ

תוּ תָ תֶ תֵי תוֹ

Please help the letters find the animals.

START !

END

END

START

© LINDA SAMUELS